THE VANCOUVER SUN

thebest

cookies and
bars *and Christmas baking*

FEATURING CANADA'S BEST-SELLING AUTHORS FROM *THE VANCOUVER SUN* TEST KITCHEN

RUTH PHELAN AND BRENDA THOMPSON

Published by
Pacific Newspaper Group, A CanWest Company
1 - 200 Granville Street
Vancouver, B.C.
V6C 3N3

Pacific Newspaper Group President and Publisher:
   Dennis Skulsky

Phelan, Ruth
   The Best Cookies and Bars and Christmas Baking / Ruth Phelan and Brenda Thompson.
Includes Index.
ISBN 1-55285-639-9

Design:	Kelly Bagshaw, Fleming Design
Production Designer:	Betty Smith, Fleming Design
Photography:	All photos by Peter Battistoni except:

   Whaletown Cookies, Ian Smith
   Triple Chocolate Hazelnut Brownies, Mark Van Manen
   Jumbleberry Oatmeal Crumb Bars, Ian Lindsay
   Vanilla Bean Shortbread Wedges, Steve Bosch
   Chocolate Hazelnut Shortbread Stars, Denise Howard

Home Economists:	Ruth Phelan
	Brenda Thompson
Nutritional Analysis:	Jean Fremont
Index:	Lucia Jamieson
Editor:	Shelley Fralic

Printed and bound in Canada by Transcontinental Printing

Distributed by: Whitecap Books Ltd.
                351 Lynn Avenue
                North Vancouver, B.C. V7J 2C4

Introduction

This cookbook is a collection of some of the best recipes for bars, cookies and Christmas baking ever to come out of *The Vancouver Sun* Test Kitchen.

All 47 recipes are our five-star winners. Some reflect modern trends and tastes while others are Test Kitchen favourites that have remained popular with readers for decades.

You'll notice that chocolate and ginger figure prominently in many of the recipes — they're our weakness — while other wonderful ingredients like oatmeal and dried fruit provide a great balance of variety and flavour for adults and children alike.

For those bakers who enjoy using upscale ingredients, we have included recipes using macadamia nuts, vanilla beans and even lavender flowers, for special occasions.

We know that your time is at a premium these days and that you can't always do as much baking as your mother or grandmother may have done.

But we hope this cookbook inspires you to spend a bit more time in the kitchen, perhaps establishing some new family traditions of your own.

Ruth Phelan
Brenda Thompson
Vancouver, B.C.
November, 2004

A Baker's Guide to the Recipes

- To melt chocolate, put chocolate in heatproof bowl set over saucepan of hot, not simmering, water until chocolate is about three-quarters melted (water should not touch the bottom of bowl), stirring occassionally. Remove bowl from saucepan and continue stirring until melted and smooth.

- Crystallized ginger: Buy Australian chunky, it's darker in colour and has a more peppery flavour than the thinner, paler slices of crystallized ginger that are heavily coated with coarse sugar.

- Preserved ginger is similar to crystallized ginger but instead of being coated with sugar, the translucent pieces of ginger are packed in a jar with syrup. Both the ginger and syrup can be used to flavour sweet and savoury dishes.

- To toast hazelnuts, spread nuts on rimmed baking sheet and bake at 350 F (180 C) for 8 to 10 minutes or until fragrant and lightly browned. Transfer nuts to tea towel; roll nuts around, inside towel, to remove as much of the hazelnut skins as possible.

- To toast pecans, spread nuts on rimmed baking sheet and bake at 350 F (180 C) for 6 to 8 minutes or until fragrant and lightly browned.

- Storing cookies: Layer cookies between sheets of wax paper in airtight container and store at room temperature for up to 3 days (2 weeks for shortbread) or freeze for up to 2 weeks (1 month for shortbread).

- Storing bars: Unless specified otherwise, cover pan of bars tightly with plastic wrap and store at room temperature for up to 2 days or transfer to airtight container and freeze for up to 2 weeks.

- Beating or stirring: When the recipe instructions specify "beat" ingredients, this should be done with an electric mixer. "Stirring" is done by hand with a wooden or metal spoon.

- Butter is salted.

Anise Fig Biscotti (recipe on following page)

Cookies

Anise Fig Biscotti

1¾   cups (425 mL) plus 2 tablespoons (30 mL) all-purpose flour

2   teaspoons (10 mL) anise seeds, crushed

2   teaspoons (10 mL) baking powder

¼   teaspoon (1 mL) salt

2   large eggs

¾   cup (175 mL) granulated sugar

⅓   cup (75 mL) butter, melted

¼   teaspoon (1 mL) vanilla extract

2   tablespoons (30 mL) finely grated lemon zest

¾   cup (175 mL) coarsely chopped dried figs

In large bowl, combine flour, anise seeds, baking powder and salt. In medium bowl, whisk together eggs, sugar, butter, vanilla and zest; stir in figs. Add to flour mixture and stir until soft, sticky dough forms. Transfer dough to floured surface. With lightly floured hands, knead dough until it comes together. (Dough will be sticky.)

Divide dough in half and transfer to parchment-paper-lined baking sheet. With lightly floured hands, shape each half into a flat log, 10 inches (25 cm) long and 2½ inches (6 cm) wide, leaving 3 inches (7 cm) between logs.

Bake at 325 F (160 C) for 25 to 28 minutes or until golden and firm to the touch. Place baking sheet on rack and let logs cool for 5 minutes, then transfer to cutting board. Using serrated knife, cut each log diagonally into ¾-inch (2 cm) thick slices.

Stand slices upright, not touching one another, on parchment-paper-lined baking sheet. Bake for 25 to 30 minutes or until golden. Transfer slices to rack and let cool.

Makes 20 biscotti. PER BISCOTTO: 112 cal, 2 g pro, 4 g fat, 18 g carb.

Over-The-Top Chocoholics' Cookies

1	pound (500 g) bittersweet chocolate, chopped (3 cups/750 mL)
½	cup (125 mL) all-purpose flour
1	teaspoon (5 mL) baking powder
¼	teaspoon (1 mL) salt
1	teaspoon (5 mL) dark roast instant coffee granules
1 ½	cups (375 mL) granulated sugar
4	large eggs
¼	cup (50 mL) butter, melted
2	teaspoons (10 mL) vanilla extract
11	ounces (300 g) white chocolate, chopped coarse (about 2 cups/500 mL)
¾	cup (175 mL) pecans, toasted and chopped coarse

Melt bittersweet chocolate and set aside to cool slightly. In small bowl, combine flour, baking powder and salt.

Rub coffee granules between fingertips to form a powder. In large bowl, beat sugar and eggs for 5 minutes or until pale yellow and thick. Beat in melted bittersweet chocolate, butter, vanilla and coffee powder. Add flour mixture, stirring until just blended. Stir in white chocolate and pecans. Cover tightly and refrigerate dough for 45 minutes or until firm.

Drop dough by ¼ cupfuls (50 mL), 2 inches (5 cm) apart, onto parchment-paper-lined rimless baking sheets. Using moist fingertips, press top of each cookie to form 2½-inch (6 cm) round.

Bake at 350 F (180 C) for 10 to 12 minutes or until tops become dry and crack (centres will be soft). Let cookies cool on baking sheet for 3 minutes, then transfer to rack and let cool.

Tip: Parchment paper prevents the chocolate from scorching.

Makes 25 cookies. PER COOKIE: 271 cal, 4 g pro, 17 g fat, 32 g carb.

Pistachio Chocolate Chip Cookies

1 ¼	cups (300 mL) all-purpose flour
½	teaspoon (2 mL) baking soda
¼	teaspoon (1 mL) salt
⅓	cup (75 mL) quick-cooking oats (not instant)
½	cup (125 mL) butter, at room temperature
½	cup (125 mL) packed brown sugar
¼	cup (50 mL) granulated sugar
1	large egg
1	teaspoon (5 mL) vanilla extract
1	cup (250 mL) white chocolate chips
¾	cup (175 mL) shelled unsalted pistachios, chopped (divided)

In small bowl, combine flour, soda, salt and oats. In large bowl, beat butter, brown sugar and granulated sugar until fluffy. Beat in egg and vanilla. Add flour mixture, stirring until just blended. Stir in white chocolate chips and ½ cup (125 mL) pistachios.

Drop dough by heaping teaspoonfuls (5 mL), 2½ inches (6 cm) apart, onto greased rimless baking sheets. Using fork, press top of each cookie until ½-inch (1 cm) thick and sprinkle with about ¼ teaspoon (1 mL) of remaining pistachios; press lightly with fingertips.

Bake at 350 F (180 C) for 8 to 10 minutes or until light golden. (For chewy cookies, do not overbake.) Let cookies cool on baking sheet for 1 minute, then transfer to rack and let cool.

Tip: If you can't find shelled pistachios, buy about 7 ounces (200 g) of pistachios in the shell to yield ¾ cup (175 mL) shelled.

Makes 36 cookies. PER COOKIE: 99 cal, 2 g pro, 6 g fat, 11 g carb.

Dried Fruit Oatmeal Cookies

3 ½	cups (875 mL) all-purpose flour
1	teaspoon (5 mL) baking soda
1	teaspoon (5 mL) cream of tartar
1	teaspoon (5 mL) salt
1	cup (250 mL) butter, at room temperature
¾	cup (175 mL) vegetable oil
1	cup (250 mL) packed brown sugar
1	cup (250 mL) granulated sugar
2	large eggs
1	teaspoon (5 mL) vanilla extract
2	cups (500 mL) quick-cooking oats (not instant)
1	cup (250 mL) crisp rice cereal
1	cup (250 mL) dried blueberries
¾	cup (175 mL) chopped dried peaches

In medium bowl, combine flour, soda, cream of tartar and salt.

In large bowl, beat butter, oil, brown sugar and granulated sugar until well blended. Add eggs and vanilla; beat well. Add flour mixture, one-third at a time, stirring until just blended. Stir in oats, cereal, blueberries and peaches.

Drop by heaping teaspoonfuls (5 mL), 2 inches (5 cm) apart, onto parchment-paper-lined or ungreased rimless baking sheets and flatten slightly with fork.

Bake at 350 F (180 C) for 12 to 14 minutes or until light golden. Transfer cookies to rack and let cool.

Tip: Substitute dried cranberries for blueberries, or dried apples for peaches.

Makes 66 cookies. PER COOKIE: 120 cal, 2.g pro, 6 g fat, 16 g carb.

Tart Cherry Almond Cookies

1 ¼	cups (300 mL) all-purpose flour
½	teaspoon (2 mL) baking soda
½	teaspoon (2 mL) salt
½	cup (125 mL) butter, at room temperature
¾	cup (175 mL) packed brown sugar
¼	cup (50 mL) granulated sugar
2	large eggs
1	teaspoon (5 mL) almond extract
5	ounces (140 g) white chocolate, chopped coarse
1	cup (250 mL) coarsely chopped dried tart cherries (about 5 ounces/140 g)
1	cup (250 mL) sliced natural almonds
½	cup (125 mL) sweetened flaked coconut

In small bowl, combine flour, soda and salt. In large bowl, beat butter, brown sugar and granulated sugar until fluffy. Beat in eggs, one at a time, beating well after each addition. Beat in almond extract. Add flour mixture, stirring until just blended. Stir in chocolate, cherries, almonds and coconut.

Drop dough by heaping tablespoonfuls (15 mL), 2 inches (5 cm) apart, onto parchment-paper-lined or greased rimless baking sheets.

Bake at 350 F (180 C) for 12 to 14 minutes or until golden. Transfer cookies to rack and let cool.

Tip: *It's worth taking the time to seek out dried tart cherries. Dried sweet cherries are widely available but tart cherries impart a distinct tangy flavour. You can substitute dried cranberries, if desired.*

Makes 32 cookies. PER COOKIE: 133 cal, 2 g pro, 7 g fat, 17 g carb.

Almond Biscotti

1 ¾   cups (425 mL) plus 2 tablespoons (30 mL) all-purpose flour
2   teaspoons (10 mL) baking powder
¼   teaspoon (1 mL) salt
¾   cup (175 mL) natural almonds, chopped coarse
2   large eggs
½   cup (125 mL) granulated sugar
¼   cup (50 mL) butter, melted
1   tablespoon (15 mL) liquid honey
1   tablespoon (15 mL) finely grated orange zest
1   teaspoon (5 mL) vanilla extract
½   teaspoon (2 mL) almond extract

In large bowl, combine flour, baking powder, salt and almonds. In medium bowl, whisk together eggs, sugar, butter, honey, zest, vanilla and almond extract. Add to flour mixture and stir until soft, sticky dough forms. Transfer dough to floured surface. With lightly floured hands, knead dough until it comes together. (Dough will be sticky.)

Divide dough in half and transfer to parchment-paper-lined baking sheet. With lightly floured hands, shape each half into a flat log, 10 inches (25 cm) long and 2½ inches (6 cm) wide, leaving 3 inches (7 cm) between logs.

Bake at 325 F (160 C) for 25 to 28 minutes or until golden and firm to the touch. Place baking sheet on rack and let logs cool for 5 minutes, then transfer to cutting board. Using serrated knife, cut each log diagonally into ¾-inch (2 cm) thick slices. Stand slices upright, not touching one another, on parchment-paper-lined baking sheet. Bake for 25 minutes or until golden. Transfer slices to rack and let cool.

Tip: Omit almond extract and increase vanilla by ¼ teaspoon (1 mL).

Makes 20 biscotti. PER BISCOTTO: 122 cal, 3 g pro, 5 g fat, 16 g carb.

Dad's Cookies

2 ½	cups (625 mL) quick-cooking oats (not instant)
2	cups (500 mL) all-purpose flour
1	teaspoon (5 mL) baking soda
½	teaspoon (2 mL) salt
¾	teaspoon (4 mL) ground ginger
½	teaspoon (2 mL) ground allspice
½	teaspoon (2 mL) ground cinnamon
1	cup (250 mL) vegetable shortening
1 ¼	cups (300 mL) granulated sugar
2	large eggs
½	cup (125 mL) golden corn syrup
1	cup (250 mL) unsweetened medium coconut

Finely grind oats in blender or food processor; measure 2 cups (500 mL). In medium bowl, combine flour, soda, salt, ginger, allspice and cinnamon.

In large bowl, beat shortening and sugar until well blended. Add eggs, one at a time, beating well after each addition. Beat in corn syrup. Add flour mixture, stirring until just blended. Stir in coconut and ground oats. Shape dough into 1-inch (2.5 cm) balls and place, 3 inches (7 cm) apart, on parchment-paper-lined or greased rimless baking sheets.

Bake at 325 F (160 C) for 18 to 22 minutes or until golden. Let cookies cool on sheet for 2 minutes, then transfer to rack and let cool.

Tip: *Butter can be substituted for shortening. Instead of shaping the dough into balls, drop it by tablespoonfuls (15 mL) onto prepared baking sheets. Cookies will be larger and thinner than ones made with shortening.*

Makes 72 cookies. PER COOKIE: 99 cal, 1 g pro, 5 g fat, 13 g carb.

Whaletown Cookies

2	cups (500 mL) all-purpose flour
1	teaspoon (5 mL) baking powder
½	teaspoon (2 mL) baking soda
¼	teaspoon (1 mL) salt
1	cup (250 mL) vegetable shortening
2	cups (500 mL) packed brown sugar
2	large eggs
1	teaspoon (5 mL) vanilla extract
1	cup (250 mL) quick-cooking oats (not instant)
1	cup (250 mL) unsweetened medium coconut

In medium bowl, combine flour, baking powder, soda and salt.

In large bowl, beat shortening and sugar until well blended. Add eggs, one at a time, beating well after each addition. Beat in vanilla. Add flour mixture, one-third at a time, stirring until just blended. Stir in oats and coconut.

Shape dough into 1½-inch (4 cm) balls and place, 3 inches (7 cm) apart, on parchment-paper-lined or greased rimless baking sheets. Flatten each ball with fork.

Bake at 350 F (180 C) for 12 to 15 minutes or until golden. Let cookies cool on baking sheet for 2 minutes, then transfer to rack and let cool.

Tip: *Back when this old favourite recipe first appeared in* The Vancouver Sun *in 1947, vegetable shortening was used. Nowadays, people prefer to use butter. Substitute butter, and the cookies will be larger and thinner than the ones made with shortening.*

Makes 42 cookies. PER COOKIE: 136 cal, 1 g pro, 7 g fat, 17 g carb.

Lavender Lemon Shortbread

3 ¼   cups (800 mL) all-purpose flour, divided
½   cup (125 mL) cornstarch
2   tablespoons (30 mL) finely chopped fresh lavender flowers
2   cups (500 mL) butter, at room temperature
1   cup (250 mL) icing sugar
2   teaspoons (10 mL) finely grated lemon zest
2   ounces (60 g) white chocolate, chopped
1   teaspoon (5 mL) vegetable oil

In medium bowl, combine 3 cups (750 mL) flour, cornstarch and lavender. In large bowl, beat butter, sugar and zest until fluffy. Add flour mixture, one-third at a time, beating until just blended.

Turn dough out onto lightly floured surface and gradually knead in remaining ¼ cup (50 mL) flour to make a soft, smooth dough.

Using small spatula, press dough evenly into ungreased 13x9-inch (33x23 cm) baking pan and prick all over with fork. Refrigerate for 45 minutes.

Bake at 300 F (150 C) for 55 minutes or until pale golden, covering pan loosely with foil for the last 5 minutes of baking time. Place pan on rack and lightly score top of shortbread into 24 bars. Let shortbread stand in pan on rack until cool.

Melt chocolate with oil. Using fork, drizzle chocolate over shortbread; let chocolate set. Following score marks, cut shortbread into bars.

Tip: *Some varieties of lavender are intensely flavoured and imbue a perfume scent. We used the delicate, pleasant smelling, sweet English lavender for these bars.*

Makes 24 cookies. PER COOKIE: 251 cal, 2 g pro, 17 g fat, 22 g carb.

Oh-So-Zesty Crisp Lemon Cookies

2	cups (500 mL) all-purpose flour
¼	teaspoon (1 mL) baking soda
½	teaspoon (2 mL) salt
1	cup (250 mL) butter, at room temperature
½	cup (125 mL) packed brown sugar
½	cup (125 mL) granulated sugar
1	large egg
½	teaspoon (2 mL) vanilla extract
2	tablespoons (30 mL) finely grated lemon zest
1	tablespoon (15 mL) fresh lemon juice
	Granulated sugar

In medium bowl, combine flour, soda and salt. In large bowl, beat butter, brown sugar and ½ cup (125 mL) granulated sugar until fluffy. Beat in egg, then vanilla, zest and lemon juice until well blended. Add flour mixture, one-third at a time, stirring until just blended.

Divide dough in half. On lightly floured surface, shape each half into a roll, 7 inches (18 cm) long and 1¾ inches (4.5 cm) in diameter. Wrap each roll in plastic wrap and refrigerate overnight.

Remove dough rolls, one at a time, from refrigerator; using knife with a sharp thin blade, cut into ¼-inch (5 mm) thick slices. Place each slice, 2 inches (5 cm) apart, on parchment-paper-lined or greased rimless baking sheets. Lightly sprinkle each slice with granulated sugar.

Bake at 350 F (180 C) for 10 to 12 minutes or until light golden around edges. Transfer cookies to rack and let cool.

Tip: *One large lemon yields about 4 teaspoons (20 mL) finely grated lemon zest and 4 tablespoons (60 mL) fresh lemon juice.*

Makes 56 cookies. PER COOKIE: 64 cal, 1 g pro, 4 g fat, 8 g carb.

Halloween Sugar Cookies

Cookies

3 ½	cups (875 mL) all-purpose flour
2	teaspoons (10 mL) cream of tartar
1	teaspoon (5 mL) baking soda
1	cup (250 mL) butter, at room temperature
1	cup (250 mL) granulated sugar
2	large eggs
1 ½	teaspoons (7 mL) vanilla extract

Icing

4	cups (1 L) icing sugar
¼	cup (50 mL) butter, at room temperature
4	tablespoons (60 mL) milk, about
	Black and orange food colouring

Cookies: In medium bowl, combine flour, cream of tartar and soda. In large bowl, beat butter and granulated sugar until fluffy. Add eggs, one at a time, beating well after each addition. Beat in vanilla. Add flour mixture, one-third at a time, stirring until just blended.

Divide dough in half; flatten each piece into a round, about ¾-inch (2 cm) thick. Wrap each round completely in plastic wrap and refrigerate overnight or until well chilled.

Roll out each round of dough on lightly floured surface until just slightly less than ¼-inch (5 mm) thick. Using 3-inch (7 cm) Halloween cookie cutters, cut into shapes. Place on parchment-paper-lined or greased rimless baking sheets.

Bake at 375 F (190 C) for 8 to 10 minutes or until light golden on bottom and edges. Transfer cookies to rack and let cool. *(Make-ahead: Cooled cookies can be layered between sheets of wax paper in airtight container and frozen for up to 2 weeks. Thaw in container before icing.)*

Icing: In large bowl, beat together icing sugar, butter and 3 tablespoons (45 mL) of the milk. Beat in enough of the remaining milk to make icing of spreading consistency. Tint icing with desired food colouring. Spread cookies with a thin layer of icing and let set.

Tips

- *Check out specialty cookware shops for hard-to-find food colouring pastes to colour icing.*
- *We tested several sugar cookies before deciding on this one from* The Vancouver Sun's Edith Adams Cottage Christmas Baking Book *(now out of print)— it had less sugar than the others. If you don't want to ice the cookies, lightly sprinkle unbaked cookies with granulated sugar before baking.*

Makes 50 cookies. PER COOKIE: 126 cal, 1 g pro, 5 g fat, 20 g carb.

Spooky Crispy Creatures

⅓	cup (75 mL) butter, at room temperature
1	(85 g) package orange jelly powder
1	(250 g) package miniature marshmallows
6	cups (1.5 L) crisp rice cereal
	Icing and candies for decoration, optional

Grease 15½x10½x1-inch (39x27x2.5 cm) jelly roll pan.

In large heavy saucepan, melt butter over low heat. Add jelly powder and stir until blended. Add marshmallows; stir until melted and blended. Remove from heat and quickly stir in cereal until well coated.

Scrape mixture into prepared pan. With lightly buttered spatula, spread evenly in pan and press until level. Refrigerate for 20 minutes or until chilled.

Using 3-inch (7 cm) metal Halloween cookie cutters, cut shapes out of cereal mixture. To protect your hand, wear an oven mitt when pressing cookie cutters into cereal mixture. If desired, decorate with icing and candy pieces.

Microwave Method: In large bowl, microwave butter on High for about 40 seconds or until melted. Stir in jelly powder, then marshmallows. Microwave on High for about 1½ minutes or until marshmallows melt, stirring after 45 seconds. Quickly stir in cereal.

Tip: One (250 g) package miniature marshmallows yields 5 cups (1.25 L).

Makes 24 cookies. PER COOKIE: 96 cal, 1 g pro, 3 g fat, 18 g carb.

Chewy Coconut Macaroons

3 ½	cups (875 mL) sweetened flaked coconut
⅓	cup (75 mL) all-purpose flour
¼	teaspoon (1 mL) salt
½	cup (125 mL) chopped candied (glacé) orange peel
1	(300 mL) can sweetened condensed partially skimmed milk
2	teaspoons (10 mL) vanilla extract

In large bowl, combine coconut, flour, salt and orange peel. Stir in condensed milk and vanilla. Drop heaping tablespoonfuls (15 mL), 2 inches (5 cm) apart, onto parchment-paper-lined baking sheets.

Bake at 325 F (160 C) for 15 minutes or until golden around edges and lightly tinged with brown on top. Let cool on baking sheet for 2 minutes, then transfer cookies to rack and let cool.

Variation: Substitute ¼ cup (50 mL) sliced natural almonds and ¼ cup (50 mL) semi-sweet chocolate chips for the candied orange peel.

Tips

- *Don't be tempted to use low-fat sweetened condensed partially skimmed milk — the macaroons will spread too much while baking.*
- *To measure flour, stir and lightly spoon flour into a dry measuring cup until filled slightly above the rim; level off with the straight edge of a knife. (Do not shake or tap cup, this will increase the amount of flour in cup.)*

Makes 28 cookies. PER COOKIE: 88 cal, 2 g pro, 4 g fat, 13 g carb.

Three Ginger Bar Cookies

2 ¼	cups (550 mL) all-purpose flour
1	teaspoon (5 mL) baking soda
½	teaspoon (2 mL) salt
2	teaspoons (10 mL) ground ginger
¾	cup (175 mL) butter, at room temperature
1	cup (250 mL) packed brown sugar
¼	cup (50 mL) fancy molasses
1	large egg
4	teaspoons (20 mL) finely chopped fresh ginger
½	cup (125 mL) finely chopped crystallized ginger

In medium bowl, combine flour, soda, salt and ground ginger.

In large bowl, beat butter and sugar until fluffy. Beat in molasses, then egg and fresh ginger. Add flour mixture and stir until just blended. Add crystallized ginger and stir until well mixed.

Drop mounds of dough over entire surface of greased 15½x10½x1-inch (39x27x2.5 cm) jelly roll pan. Using fingertips, press dough evenly in pan and smooth surface with metal spatula.

Bake at 350 F (180 C) for 13 to 15 minutes or until lightly browned. Let cool in pan on rack for 15 minutes, then cut into bars. Transfer bar cookies to rack and let cool.

Makes 40 cookies. PER COOKIE: 93 cal, 1 g pro, 4 g fat, 15 g carb.

Triple Chocolate Chunk Bar Cookies

1 ¼   cups (300 mL) all-purpose flour
½   teaspoon (2 mL) baking soda
⅛   teaspoon (0.5 mL) salt
½   cup (125 mL) butter, at room temperature
½   cup (125 mL) packed brown sugar
⅓   cup (75 mL) granulated sugar
1   large egg
1   teaspoon (5 mL) vanilla extract
½   cup (125 mL) bittersweet chocolate chunks (¼-inch/5 mm)
½   cup (125 mL) white chocolate chunks (¼-inch/5 mm)
½   cup (125 mL) milk chocolate chunks (¼-inch/5 mm)
½   cup (125 mL) pecans, chopped

In small bowl, combine flour, soda and salt.

In large bowl, beat butter, brown sugar and granulated sugar until fluffy.
Beat in egg and vanilla. Add flour mixture and stir until just blended.
Stir in bittersweet, white and milk chocolate chunks, and pecans.

Drop mounds of dough over entire surface of parchment-paper-lined
15½x10½x1-inch (39x27x2.5 cm) jelly roll pan. Using fingertips, press
dough evenly in pan and smooth surface with metal spatula.

Bake at 300 F (150 C) for 20 minutes or until golden around edges.
Let cool in pan on rack for 15 minutes, then cut into bars. Transfer bar
cookies to rack and let cool.

Tip: To store chocolate, wrap in foil first, then wrap in plastic wrap and
place in airtight container. Store in cool, dry place.

Makes 40 cookies. PER COOKIE: 81 cal, 1 g pro, 4 g fat, 11 g carb.

Spicy Pear Ginger Cookies

2	cups (500 mL) all-purpose flour
¾	teaspoon (4 mL) baking powder
¾	teaspoon (4 mL) baking soda
¼	teaspoon (1 mL) salt
¾	teaspoon (4 mL) ground cinnamon
½	teaspoon (2 mL) ground ginger
½	teaspoon (2 mL) ground nutmeg
⅛	teaspoon (0.5 mL) ground cloves
½	cup (125 mL) butter, at room temperature
1 ¼	cups (300 mL) packed dark brown sugar
1	large egg
⅓	cup (75 mL) fancy molasses
1	cup (250 mL) coarsely chopped dried pears
½	cup (125 mL) pecans, chopped coarse
1	tablespoon (15 mL) finely chopped crystallized ginger

In medium bowl, combine flour, baking powder, soda, salt, cinnamon, ground ginger, nutmeg and cloves. In large bowl, beat butter and sugar until fluffy. Beat in egg, then molasses. Add flour mixture, stirring until just blended. Stir in pears, pecans and crystallized ginger.

Drop dough by heaping tablespoonfuls (15 mL), 2 inches (5 cm) apart, onto parchment-paper-lined rimless baking sheets.

Bake at 375 F (190 C) for 12 minutes or until edges of cookies are light golden, but centres are still quite soft. (Do not overbake.)

Let cookies cool on baking sheet for 3 minutes, then transfer to rack and let cool.

Tip: *Cut up dried pears with kitchen shears rather than a knife.*

Makes 32 cookies. PER COOKIE: 129 cal, 1 g pro, 5 g fat, 22 g carb.

Oatmeal Raisin Cookies

2	cups (500 mL) all-purpose flour
3/4	teaspoon (4 mL) baking powder
1/4	teaspoon (1 mL) baking soda
1/2	teaspoon (2 mL) salt
1/2	teaspoon (2 mL) ground cinnamon
1	cup (250 mL) butter, at room temperature
3/4	cup (175 mL) packed brown sugar
3/4	cup (175 mL) granulated sugar
2	large eggs
1	teaspoon (5 mL) vanilla extract
2	cups (500 mL) large flake (old-fashioned) or quick-cooking oats (not instant)
2	cups (500 mL) raisins
1	cup (250 mL) walnuts, chopped coarse

~ chopped

In medium bowl, combine flour, baking powder, soda, salt and cinnamon. In large bowl, beat butter, brown sugar and granulated sugar until fluffy. Add eggs, one at a time, beating well after each addition. Beat in vanilla. Add flour mixture, stirring until just blended. Stir in oats, raisins and walnuts.

Drop by heaping tablespoonfuls (15 mL), 2 inches (5 cm) apart, onto parchment-paper-lined or greased rimless baking sheets. Press lightly with fork.

Bake at 350 F (180 C) for 12 to 14 minutes or until golden and set around edges but still slightly soft in the centre. Transfer cookies to rack and let cool.

Variation: Substitute chocolate chips for walnuts.

Makes 52 cookies. PER COOKIE: 126 cal, 2 g pro, 6 g fat, 18 g carb.

Jumbo Oatmeal Cranberry Cookies

2	cups (500 mL) quick-cooking oats (not instant), divided
1 ½	cups (375 mL) all-purpose flour
1	teaspoon (5 mL) baking powder
½	teaspoon (2 mL) baking soda
½	teaspoon (2 mL) salt
1	teaspoon (5 mL) ground cinnamon
¼	teaspoon (1 mL) ground allspice
⅛	teaspoon (0.5 mL) ground cloves
1	cup (250 mL) butter, at room temperature
1	cup (250 mL) packed brown sugar
½	cup (125 mL) granulated sugar
2	large eggs
1	teaspoon (5 mL) vanilla extract
1	cup (250 mL) dried cranberries

Finely grind 1 cup (250 mL) oats in food processor. In bowl, combine flour, baking powder, soda, salt, cinnamon, allspice and cloves.

In large bowl, beat butter, brown sugar and granulated sugar until fluffy. Add eggs, one at a time, beating well after each addition. Beat in vanilla. Add flour mixture, stirring until just blended. Stir in ground oats and remaining 1 cup (250 mL) oats. Stir in cranberries.

Drop dough by level ¼ cupfuls (50 mL), 3 inches (7 cm) apart, onto parchment-paper-lined rimless baking sheets. Using fork, press each cookie until ½-inch (1 cm) thick.

Bake at 350 F (180 C) for 14 minutes or until light golden. Let cookies cool on baking sheet for 2 minutes, then transfer to rack and let cool.

Variation: Add ½ cup (125 mL) sesame seeds to dough.

Makes 18 cookies. PER COOKIE: 267 cal, 4 g pro, 12 g fat, 37 g carb.

Peanut Butter Bar Cookies

1	cup (250 mL) unsalted roasted peanuts
1 ½	cups (375 mL) all-purpose flour
¼	teaspoon (1 mL) baking powder
¼	teaspoon (1 mL) baking soda
½	teaspoon (2 mL) salt
½	cup (125 mL) butter, at room temperature
½	cup (125 mL) smooth peanut butter
½	cup (125 mL) packed brown sugar
½	cup (125 mL) granulated sugar
1	large egg
1	teaspoon (5 mL) vanilla extract
1	cup (250 mL) semi-sweet chocolate chips

Place peanuts in food processor and process until nuts are chopped coarse. In small bowl, combine flour, baking powder, soda and salt.

In large bowl, beat butter and peanut butter until well blended. Add brown sugar and granulated sugar; beat until fluffy. Beat in egg and vanilla. Add flour mixture and stir until just blended. Stir in chopped peanuts and chocolate chips.

Drop mounds of dough over entire surface of greased 15½x10½x1-inch (39x27x2.5 cm) jelly roll pan. Using fingertips, press dough evenly in pan and smooth surface with metal spatula.

Bake at 350 F (180 C) for 15 to 17 minutes or until golden around edges. Let cool in pan on rack for 15 minutes, then cut into bars. Transfer bar cookies to rack and let cool.

Tip: Use homogenized rather than natural peanut butter, which has a layer of oil on top.

Makes 40 cookies. PER COOKIE: 124 cal, 3 g pro, 8 g fat, 13 g carb.

Oat Chocolate Chip Bar Cookies

1 ¼	cups (300 mL) quick-cooking oats (not instant)
1	cup (250 mL) all-purpose flour
½	teaspoon (2 mL) baking soda
¼	teaspoon (1 mL) salt
½	cup (125 mL) butter, at room temperature
½	cup (125 mL) packed brown sugar
½	cup (125 mL) granulated sugar
1	large egg
1	teaspoon (5 mL) vanilla extract
1	cup (250 mL) milk chocolate chips
1	cup (250 mL) semi-sweet chocolate chips

Put oats in food processor and process until finely chopped. In medium bowl, combine flour, soda and salt; stir in chopped oats.

In large bowl, beat butter, brown sugar and granulated sugar until fluffy. Beat in egg and vanilla. Add flour mixture and stir until just blended. Stir in milk chocolate and semi-sweet chocolate chips.

Drop mounds of dough over entire surface of greased 15½x10½x1-inch (39x27x2.5 cm) jelly roll pan. Using fingertips, press dough evenly in pan and smooth surface with metal spatula. (Dough doesn't completely fill pan; the odd small gap will fill in when dough spreads during baking.)

Bake at 350 F (180 C) for 13 to 15 minutes or until golden around edges. Let cool in pan on rack for 15 minutes, then cut into bars. Transfer bar cookies to rack and let cool.

Tip: *Instant oats are specifically processed for instantly making into a hot cereal and do not make a good substitute for quick-cooking oats.*

Makes 40 cookies. PER COOKIE: 106 cal, 1 g pro, 5 g fat, 14 g carb.

Nutty Sunflower Seed Bar Cookies

4	cups (1 L) quick-cooking oats (not instant)
1	cup (250 mL) mini semi-sweet chocolate chips
1	cup (250 mL) dried currants
1	cup (250 mL) unsalted roasted peanuts, chopped fine
½	cup (125 mL) unsalted sunflower seeds
½	cup (125 mL) butter, at room temperature
1 ½	cups (375 mL) smooth peanut butter
1 ½	cups (375 mL) packed brown sugar
¼	cup (50 mL) golden corn syrup
1	teaspoon (5 mL) salt
2	large eggs
1	teaspoon (5 mL) vanilla extract

In large bowl, combine oats, chocolate chips, currants, peanuts and sunflower seeds.

In large heavy saucepan, combine butter and peanut butter. Place over medium-low heat; stir until butter is melted and blended with peanut butter. Remove from heat. Add sugar, corn syrup and salt; stir until blended. Whisk in eggs and vanilla.

Add peanut butter mixture to oat mixture; stir until well mixed. Press evenly into greased 15½x10½x1-inch (39x27x2.5 cm) jelly roll pan; smooth surface with metal spatula.

Bake at 350 F (180 C) for 23 minutes or until golden around edges and just barely set in middle. Let cool in pan on rack. Cut into bars.

Tip: *Use homogenized rather than natural peanut butter, which has a layer of oil on top.*

Makes 21 cookies. PER COOKIE: 352 cal, 11 g pro, 20 g fat, 39 g carb. Excellent source of niacin and magnesium. High in fibre.

Slice-of-Romance Bars (recipe on following page)

Bars

Slice-of-Romance Bars

Base

1 ¾	cups (425 mL) graham wafer crumbs
½	cup (125 mL) unsweetened medium coconut
½	cup (125 mL) pecans, toasted and chopped
½	cup (125 mL) butter, at room temperature
¼	cup (50 mL) granulated sugar
⅓	cup (75 mL) unsweetened cocoa powder
1	large egg, beaten

Filling

⅓	cup (75 mL) canned whole cranberry sauce
2	cups (500 mL) icing sugar
2	tablespoons (30 mL) cornstarch
	Pinch salt
¼	cup (50 mL) butter, at room temperature
2	teaspoons (10 mL) milk
¼	teaspoon (1 mL) vanilla extract

Topping

5	ounces (140 g) semi-sweet chocolate, chopped
1	tablespoon (15 mL) butter, at room temperature
1	ounce (30 g) white chocolate, chopped
½	teaspoon (2 mL) vegetable oil

Base: In medium bowl, combine crumbs, coconut and pecans. In medium-size heavy saucepan, combine butter, granulated sugar, cocoa powder and egg. Place over low heat and cook for 6 to 8 minutes or until smooth and slightly thickened, stirring constantly. Remove from heat and stir in crumb mixture. Press evenly into greased 9-inch (23 cm) square baking pan. Refrigerate for 60 minutes or until chilled.

Filling: In blender, puree cranberry sauce until smooth and measure 3 level tablespoons (45 mL); set aside.

In large bowl, combine icing sugar, cornstarch and salt until well blended. Add 3 tablespoons (45 mL) cranberry puree, butter, milk and vanilla; beat until well blended. Spread evenly over base; cover pan tightly with plastic wrap and refrigerate for 2 hours or until firm.

Topping: Melt semi-sweet chocolate with butter. Spread evenly over chilled filling. Refrigerate for 30 minutes or until chocolate is firm.

Melt white chocolate with oil. Using fork, drizzle white chocolate over top of semi-sweet chocolate. Refrigerate for 30 minutes or until chocolate is firm. *(To store: Cover pan tightly and refrigerate for up to 3 days or transfer to airtight container and freeze for up to 2 weeks.)* When ready to serve, remove from refrigerator and let stand at room temperature for 15 minutes, then cut into bars.

Tips

* *Splurge and use premium chocolate — besides the wonderful flavour it's also easier to spread when melted.*
* *To prevent icing sugar from flying out of bowl be sure to keep electric mixer on low when starting to beat filling mixture.*

Makes 24 bars. PER BAR: 210 cal, 2 g pro, 13 g fat, 25 g carb.

Espresso Hazelnut Nanaimo Bars

Base

1 ¾	cups (425 mL) graham wafer crumbs
½	cup (125 mL) unsweetened medium coconut
½	cup (125 mL) hazelnuts, toasted and chopped
½	cup (125 mL) butter, at room temperature
¼	cup (50 mL) granulated sugar
⅓	cup (75 mL) unsweetened cocoa powder
1	large egg, beaten

Filling

1	teaspoon (5 mL) instant espresso coffee powder
1	tablespoon (15 mL) hot water
1	tablespoon (15 mL) hazelnut syrup
2	cups (500 mL) icing sugar
2	tablespoons (30 mL) cornstarch
	Pinch salt
¼	cup (50 mL) butter, at room temperature
2	tablespoons (30 mL) milk
¼	teaspoon (1 mL) vanilla extract

Topping

5	ounces (140 g) semi-sweet chocolate, chopped
1	tablespoon (15 mL) butter, at room temperature

Base: In medium bowl, combine crumbs, coconut and hazelnuts. In medium-size heavy saucepan, combine butter, granulated sugar, cocoa powder and egg. Place over low heat and cook for 6 to 8 minutes or until smooth and slightly thickened, stirring constantly. Remove from heat and stir in crumb mixture. Press evenly into greased 9-inch (23 cm) square baking pan. Refrigerate for 60 minutes or until chilled.

Filling: In small bowl, dissolve coffee powder in hot water. Stir in syrup and let cool.

In large bowl, combine icing sugar, cornstarch and salt until well blended. Add coffee mixture, butter, milk and vanilla; beat until well blended. Spread evenly over base; cover pan tightly with plastic wrap and refrigerate for 2 hours or until firm.

Topping: Melt chocolate with butter. Spread evenly over chilled filling. Refrigerate for 30 minutes or until chocolate is firm. *(To store: Cover pan tightly and refrigerate for up to 3 days or transfer to airtight container and freeze for up to 2 weeks.)* When ready to serve, remove from refrigerator and let stand at room temperature for 15 minutes, then cut into bars.

Tips

- *Not all hazelnut syrups are created equal. There are several brands of this syrup — some coffee shops sell bottles of flavoured syrups so try your favourite hangout.*
- *Instant espresso coffee powder is difficult to find — check specialty food stores and Italian delis. If you can't locate any in your area, substitute instant coffee, making sure to rub granules between fingertips to form a powder.*

Makes 24 bars. PER BAR: 201 cal, 2 g pro, 13 g fat, 23 g carb.

Espresso Toffee Bar Brownies

4	ounces (125 g) unsweetened chocolate, chopped
½	cup (125 mL) butter, at room temperature
1	teaspoon (5 mL) instant espresso coffee powder
¾	cup (175 mL) all-purpose flour
¼	teaspoon (1 mL) salt
1 ¼	cups (300 mL) granulated sugar
1	teaspoon (5 mL) vanilla extract
3	large eggs
½	cup (125 mL) pecans, chopped
3	(39 g) chocolate-covered toffee bars, chopped (Skor bars)

Melt chocolate and butter with coffee powder. Let cool slightly.

In small bowl, combine flour and salt. In large bowl, beat sugar, vanilla and melted chocolate mixture until blended. Add eggs, one at time, beating well after each addition. Beat in flour mixture. Stir in pecans and toffee bars. Spread evenly in greased 8-inch (20 cm) square baking pan.

Bake at 325 F (160 C) for 35 minutes or until almost set in centre. Let cool in pan on rack. Cut into bars.

Tip: You can buy packages of Skor toffee bits but for best results use the chocolate-covered toffee bars in this recipe.

Makes 16 bars. PER BAR: 251 cal, 3 g pro, 16 g fat, 28 g carb.

Triple Chocolate Hazelnut Brownies

2	ounces (60 g) bittersweet chocolate, chopped coarse
½	cup (125 mL) butter, at room temperature
⅔	cup (150 mL) all-purpose flour
	Pinch salt
2	large eggs
1	cup (250 mL) granulated sugar
1	teaspoon (5 mL) vanilla extract
1 ¼	cups (300 mL) hazelnuts, toasted and chopped
2	ounces (60 g) milk chocolate, chopped coarse
2	ounces (60 g) white chocolate, chopped coarse

Melt bittersweet chocolate with butter. Let cool slightly. In small bowl, combine flour and salt.

In large bowl, beat eggs until light and frothy. Gradually beat in sugar; beat in vanilla. Fold in melted bittersweet chocolate until not quite incorporated. Fold in flour mixture until not quite incorporated. Add hazelnuts, milk chocolate and white chocolate; fold in until just blended. Spread evenly in greased 8-inch (20 cm) square baking pan.

Bake at 350 F (180 C) for 30 to 35 minutes or until top is dry but toothpick inserted in centre comes out with a few moist crumbs. Run knife around edges of brownie. Cool in pan on rack. Cut into bars.

For Cookies: Cover dough tightly; refrigerate overnight. Drop dough (it will be stiff) by heaping tablespoonfuls (15 mL), 2½ inches (6 cm) apart, onto parchment-paper-lined rimless baking sheets. Bake at 325 F (160 C) for 12 minutes or until slightly set (centres will be soft). Let cool on sheet for 3 minutes, then transfer cookies to rack; let cool. Makes 34 cookies.

Makes 15 bars. PER BAR: 282 cal, 4 g pro, 20 g fat, 27 g carb.

Apple Caramel Crumb Bars

Caramel sauce

3	tablespoons (45 mL) butter
½	cup (125 mL) packed brown sugar
3	tablespoons (45 mL) granulated sugar
½	cup (125 mL) light cream
1	teaspoon (5 mL) brandy

Base

1 ¾	cups (425 mL) all-purpose flour
⅓	cup (75 mL) granulated sugar
½	teaspoon (2 mL) salt
2	teaspoons (10 mL) finely grated lemon zest
¾	cup (175 mL) cold butter, cut into small pieces
1	egg white, lightly beaten

Filling

10	cups (2.5 L) thinly sliced, peeled baking apples
¼	cup (50 mL) packed brown sugar
¼	cup (50 mL) granulated sugar
2	teaspoons (10 mL) ground cinnamon
¼	cup (50 mL) apple juice
1	tablespoon (15 mL) lemon juice
1	tablespoon (15 mL) finely grated orange zest

Topping

1 ¼	cups (300 mL) all-purpose flour
⅓	cup (75 mL) granulated sugar
½	cup (125 mL) walnuts
½	cup (125 mL) cold butter, cut into small pieces

Caramel sauce: In small heavy saucepan, combine butter, brown sugar, granulated sugar and cream. Place over medium-low heat, cook for 2 to 3 minutes or until sugar dissolves, stirring constantly. Increase heat to medium and bring sauce to a simmer, stirring frequently. Cook for 6 to 8 minutes or until slightly thickened, stirring constantly. Remove from heat and stir in brandy. Let cool.

Base: Place flour, granulated sugar, salt and lemon zest in food processor; pulse just until mixed. Scatter butter over flour mixture and process until mixture just starts to clump together. Press evenly into 13x9-inch (33x23 cm) baking pan. Brush lightly with egg white. Bake at 350 F (180 C) for 18 minutes or until light golden. Let cool on rack.

Filling: In large heavy frypan, combine apples, brown sugar, granulated sugar, cinnamon, apple juice and lemon juice. Bring to a boil over medium-high heat; cook for 18 to 20 minutes or until excess moisture has evaporated and mixture has thickened, stirring frequently. Let cool. Stir in orange zest.

Topping: Place flour and granulated sugar in food processor; pulse just until mixed. Add walnuts and scatter butter over flour mixture; process until mixture just starts to clump together. Transfer to bowl and using fingertips, squeeze together clumps of dough until the size of peas.

Spread filling evenly over base. Drizzle with half the caramel sauce. Sprinkle evenly with topping. Bake at 350 F (180 C) for 35 minutes or until light golden around edges. Let cool in pan on rack for 10 minutes. Drizzle with remaining sauce; let cool completely. Cover and refrigerate until chilled. Cut into bars. *(To store: Refrigerate for up to 2 days or transfer to airtight container and freeze for up to 2 weeks.)*

Tip: *We recommend using Spartan apples — they hold their shape well after baking. Avoid McIntosh apples — they become mushy and although the bars are divine tasting, you'll need a fork to eat them. Buy about 3 pounds (1.5 kg) of apples for this recipe.*

Makes 30 bars. PER BAR: 213 cal, 2 g pro, 11 g fat, 28 g carb.

Fatal Attraction Brownie Wedges

4	ounces (125 g) bittersweet chocolate, chopped
½	cup (125 mL) butter, at room temperature
⅔	cup (150 mL) all-purpose flour
⅛	teaspoon (0.5 mL) salt
2	large eggs
¾	cup (175 mL) granulated sugar
1	teaspoon (5 mL) vanilla extract
¾	cup (175 mL) hazelnuts, toasted and chopped coarse
2	ounces (60 g) semi-sweet chocolate, chopped coarse
	Icing sugar

Melt bittersweet chocolate with butter. Let cool slightly.

In small bowl, combine flour and salt. In large bowl, beat eggs until light and frothy. Gradually beat in granulated sugar, then vanilla. Beat in melted chocolate mixture. Fold in flour mixture until not quite incorporated. Add hazelnuts and semi-sweet chocolate; fold in until just blended. Spread evenly in greased 9-inch (23 cm) springform pan.

Bake at 350 F (180 C) for 30 minutes or until top is dry but toothpick inserted in centre comes out with a few moist crumbs. Let cool in pan on rack. Run knife around edge of brownie. Just before serving, remove side of pan and dust brownie lightly with icing sugar. Cut into wedges.

Tip: One (100 g) package of hazelnuts yields ¾ cup (175 mL).

Makes 8 wedges. PER WEDGE: 428 cal, 6 g pro, 30 g fat, 40 g carb.

Jumbleberry Oatmeal Crumb Bars

Filling

2	cups (500 mL) fresh blueberries
2	cups (500 mL) fresh raspberries
2	cups (500 mL) fresh strawberries, sliced
1	cup (250 mL) granulated sugar
¼	cup (50 mL) water
1	tablespoon (15 mL) finely grated orange zest
1	tablespoon (15 mL) orange juice

Crumb mixture

2 ½	cups (625 mL) all-purpose flour
1	teaspoon (5 mL) salt
¾	teaspoon (4 mL) baking soda
3	cups (750 mL) quick-cooking oats (not instant)
1 ¼	cups (300 mL) packed brown sugar
1 ½	cups (375 mL) butter, at room temperature
1	egg
1 ½	teaspoons (7 mL) water

Filling: In large heavy saucepan, combine blueberries, raspberries, strawberries, granulated sugar and water. Bring to a boil over medium heat and boil for 20 to 25 minutes or until thickened, stirring frequently. Stir in zest and orange juice. Transfer to heatproof bowl and let cool. *(Make-ahead: Cover bowl tightly and refrigerate for up to 3 days.)*

Crumb mixture: In large bowl, combine flour, salt and soda. Stir in oats and brown sugar until well mixed. With fork or fingertips, blend in butter until well mixed and crumbly.

Put 5 cups (1.25 L) crumb mixture into greased 13x9-inch (33x23 cm) baking pan; press evenly over bottom of pan. Bake at 350 F (180 C) for 12 minutes. Let cool on rack for 5 minutes.

In small bowl, lightly beat egg and water together. Add 2 tablespoons (30 mL) egg mixture to remaining crumb mixture and mix until clumps form. (Discard remaining egg mixture.)

Spread filling evenly over baked crumb mixture to within ¼-inch (5 mm) of sides. Sprinkle with remaining crumb mixture, breaking up any large clumps; press down lightly.

Bake at 350 F (180 C) for 35 to 40 minutes or until lightly browned. Let cool in pan on rack. Cover tightly and refrigerate until filling is chilled. Cut into bars. *(To store: Refrigerate for up to 2 days or transfer to airtight container and freeze for up to 2 weeks.)*

Tip: Frozen berries can be used in this recipe. Fire them into the saucepan directly from your freezer — no need to worry about thawing first. Just keep in mind that the extra moisture in frozen berries may cause the filling to take longer to thicken.

Blueberry Filling Variation

Substitute 6 cups (1.5 L) blueberries for berry mixture, 1 teaspoon (5 mL) finely grated lemon zest for orange zest and 2 teaspoons (10 mL) lemon juice for orange juice. (Purchase 2 pounds/1 kg blueberries and you'll have enough to make this recipe with some leftover to nibble on.)

In a pinch, omit making the prepared filling and substitute one (540 mL) can blueberry pie filling — there will be slightly less filling than if you had made it from scratch and the set will be a little softer, but it's an acceptable stand-in.

Makes 32 bars. PER BAR: 222 cal, 3 g pro, 10 g fat, 31 g carb.

Pecan Pie Squares

Base

1 ½   cups (375 mL) all-purpose flour

⅓   cup (75 mL) icing sugar

¾   cup (175 mL) cold butter, cut into small pieces

Topping

3   large eggs, whisked lightly

¾   cup (175 mL) packed brown sugar

½   cup (125 mL) golden corn syrup

2   tablespoons (30 mL) butter, melted

1   teaspoon (5 mL) vanilla extract

¼   teaspoon (1 mL) salt

1   cup (250 mL) pecans, chopped

Base: In medium bowl, combine flour and icing sugar. Using pastry blender, cut in butter until mixture resembles coarse crumbs. Press evenly onto bottom and 1-inch (2.5 cm) up sides of ungreased 9-inch (23 cm) square baking pan. Bake at 350 F (180 C) for 18 to 20 minutes or until light golden around edges. Let cool in pan on rack for 5 minutes.

Meanwhile prepare topping: In large bowl, whisk together eggs and brown sugar. Whisk in corn syrup, butter, vanilla and salt. Stir in pecans.

Pour topping evenly over warm base and bake for 30 minutes or until golden and set. Let cool in pan on rack. Cut into squares. *(To store: Cover pan tightly and refrigerate for up to 3 days or transfer to airtight container and freeze for up to 2 weeks.)*

Tip: *Pressing pastry part way up sides of baking pan prevents outside edges of filling from overbaking and crystallizing.*

Makes 16 squares. PER SQUARE: 237 cal, 3 g pro, 14 g fat, 27 g carb.

Lunchbox Granola Bars

3	cups (750 mL) quick-cooking oats (not instant)
1	cup (250 mL) crisp rice cereal
1	cup (250 mL) unsalted sunflower seeds
¼	cup (50 mL) sesame seeds
½	cup (125 mL) mini semi-sweet chocolate chips
1	cup (250 mL) finely chopped dried apricots
1	cup (250 mL) chopped dried cranberries
¾	cup (175 mL) butter, at room temperature
½	cup (125 mL) packed brown sugar
½	cup (125 mL) golden corn syrup
1 ½	teaspoons (7 mL) vanilla extract
½	teaspoon (2 mL) salt

In large bowl, combine oats, cereal, sunflower seeds, sesame seeds and chocolate chips; mix well. Add apricots and cranberries; mix well.

In another large bowl, beat butter, sugar, corn syrup, vanilla and salt until smooth. Add oat mixture and stir with spoon, then mix with hands until blended. Press evenly into greased 15½x10½x1-inch (39x27x2.5 cm) jelly roll pan, then press down firmly with spatula to smooth.

Bake at 350 F (180 C) for 25 minutes or until light golden. Let cool in pan on rack. Cut into bars. *(To store: Cover pan loosely with foil and store at room temperature for up to 2 days or transfer to airtight container and freeze for up to 2 weeks.)*

Tip: *Other dried fruit can be substituted for cranberries and apricots; try peaches, cherries or blueberries.*

Makes 30 bars. PER BAR: 178 cal, 3 g pro, 9 g fat, 24 g carb.

Wilderness Pick-Me-Up Bars

Base

2	cups (500 mL) all-purpose flour
1	cup (250 mL) quick-cooking oats (not instant)
3	tablespoons (45 mL) flax seeds, ground
¼	teaspoon (1 mL) salt
1	cup (250 mL) butter, at room temperature
¾	cup (175 mL) liquid honey
1	tablespoon (15 mL) finely grated lemon zest

Topping

2	large eggs
¼	cup (50 mL) liquid honey
1	cup (250 mL) slivered almonds
1	cup (250 mL) milk chocolate baking pieces (mini kisses)
½	cup (125 mL) chopped dried apricots
⅓	cup (75 mL) candied mixed peel
¼	cup (50 mL) chopped dried figs
¼	cup (50 mL) chopped dried papaya
¼	cup (50 mL) chopped dried pineapple
¼	cup (50 mL) unsweetened flaked coconut
¼	cup (50 mL) pepitas (raw hulled pumpkin seeds)
¼	cup (50 mL) sesame seeds

Base: In medium bowl, combine flour, oats, ground flax seeds and salt.

In large bowl, beat butter and honey until blended. Beat in zest. Add flour mixture and stir until well blended. Spread evenly in 13x9-inch (33x23 cm) baking pan.

Topping: In large bowl, beat eggs. Add honey and beat lightly until blended. In medium bowl, combine almonds, chocolate pieces, apricots, mixed peel, figs, papaya, pineapple, coconut, pepitas and sesame seeds. Add dried fruit mixture to egg mixture and stir until well coated. Spread evenly over base.

Bake at 350 F (180 C) for 30 to 35 minutes or until lightly browned. Let cool in pan on rack. Cut into bars. *(To store: Wrap bars individually in plastic wrap and refrigerate for up to 1 week or layer bars between wax paper in airtight container and freeze up to 1 month.)*

Tips

- *Flax seeds can be easily ground in a spice or coffee grinder, or blender with a narrow bottom (some of the newer blenders are too large across the bottom to successfully grind a small amount of seeds). Three tablespoons (45 mL) flax seeds will yield about ¼ cup (50 mL) ground.*
- *Don't be tempted to grate lemon zest too far ahead of time — it will lose some of its tangy flavour and fragrance. When grating, make only one or two light passes across the same surface of peel, otherwise you risk getting some of the bitter white pith below the surface.*

Makes 24 bars. PER BAR: 277 cal, 5 g pro, 15 g fat, 33 g carb.

Bake Sale Blondies

1	cup (250 mL) all-purpose flour
1	teaspoon (5 mL) baking powder
¼	teaspoon (1 mL) salt
½	cup (125 mL) butter, melted and cooled slightly
1	cup (250 mL) packed brown sugar
2	large eggs
1	teaspoon (5 mL) vanilla extract
¾	cup (175 mL) unsalted macadamia nuts, chopped
¼	cup (50 mL) butterscotch chips
1	teaspoon (5 mL) vegetable oil

In small bowl, combine flour, baking powder and salt. In large bowl, beat butter and sugar until well blended. Add eggs and vanilla; beat until blended. Add flour mixture and stir to blend. Stir in macadamia nuts. Spread evenly in greased 8-inch (20 cm) square baking pan.

Bake at 350 F (180 C) for 30 to 35 minutes or until top is dry and toothpick inserted in centre comes out with a few moist crumbs. Run knife around edge of blondies. Cool in pan on rack.

Melt butterscotch chips with oil. Using fork, drizzle melted butterscotch chips over top of blondies; let stand until set. Cut into bars.

Tip: *Due to their incredibly hard shells, macadamia nuts are usually sold already shelled. If unsalted macadamia nuts are difficult to find, substitute cashews or walnuts.*

Makes 15 bars. PER BAR: 220 cal, 3 g pro, 13 g fat, 24 g carb.

Hermit Slices

1	teaspoon (5 mL) dark roast instant coffee granules
1 ½	cups (375 mL) all-purpose flour
¾	teaspoon (4 mL) baking powder
½	teaspoon (2 mL) baking soda
¼	teaspoon (1 mL) salt
1	teaspoon (5 mL) ground cinnamon
¼	teaspoon (1 mL) ground allspice
¼	teaspoon (1 mL) ground nutmeg
⅛	teaspoon (0.5 mL) ground cloves
½	cup (125 mL) chopped dried apricots
½	cup (125 mL) chopped dried cranberries
½	cup (125 mL) chopped pitted dates
½	cup (125 mL) chopped raisins
1	cup (250 mL) walnuts, chopped
¼	cup (50 mL) finely chopped crystallized ginger
½	cup (125 mL) butter, at room temperature
1	cup (250 mL) packed brown sugar
2	large eggs

If necessary, rub coffee granules between fingertips to form a powder.

In medium bowl, combine flour, baking powder, soda, salt, coffee powder, cinnamon, allspice, nutmeg and cloves. In another medium bowl, combine apricots, cranberries, dates, raisins, walnuts and ginger; mix well.

In large bowl, beat butter and sugar until fluffy. Beat in eggs, one at a time, beating well after each addition. Add flour mixture and stir to form a soft dough. Stir in apricot mixture. Cover bowl tightly and refrigerate for 2 hours. *(Make ahead: Dough can be refrigerated overnight. Let stand at room temperature for 30 minutes before shaping into logs.)*

Line 2 rimless baking sheets with parchment paper. Divide dough into 3 equal portions. Place 2 portions of dough on 1 sheet and 1 portion of dough on the other baking sheet. Shape each portion into a flat log, 10 inches (25 cm) long, 2½ inches (6 cm) wide and ¾-inch (2 cm) thick, leaving 3 inches (7 cm) between logs.

Bake, 1 sheet at a time, at 375 F (190 C) for 16 to 18 minutes or until golden brown around edges but still slightly soft in the centre (don't over bake). Let logs cool completely on baking sheets on racks.

Transfer cooled logs to cutting board and slice each log crosswise into 6 equal pieces. *(To store: Layer slices between sheets of wax paper in airtight container and store at room temperature for up to 3 days or freeze for up to 2 weeks.)*

For Cookies: Drop unchilled dough, by heaping tablespoonfuls (15 mL), 2 inches (5 cm) apart, onto parchment-paper-lined or greased rimless baking sheets. Bake at 350 F (180 C) for 10 to 12 minutes or until golden. Transfer cookies to racks and let cool. Makes 36 cookies.

Tip: Spices tend to have a shelf life of about 6 months when stored in a cool, dark place away from sunlight. Replace them when their aroma is no longer strong. Buy spices in small quantities and purchase them from stores where there is a rapid turnover.

Makes 18 slices. PER SLICE: 243 cal, 3 g pro, 11 g fat, 36 g carb.

Pucker-Up Lemon Bars

Base

1	cup (250 mL) all-purpose flour
¼	cup (50 mL) granulated sugar
¼	cup (50 mL) ground almonds
½	cup (125 mL) cold butter, cut into small pieces

Topping

¾	cup (175 mL) granulated sugar
2	tablespoons (30 mL) all-purpose flour
½	teaspoon (2 mL) baking powder
¼	teaspoon (1 mL) salt
1	tablespoon (15 mL) finely grated lemon zest
3	tablespoons (45 mL) fresh lemon juice
2	large eggs
	Icing sugar

Base: In food processor, combine flour, granulated sugar and almonds; pulse 3 times. Add butter; process until mixture starts to cling together. Press evenly into ungreased 8-inch (20 cm) square baking pan. Bake at 350 F (180 C) for 18 minutes or until firm and edges begin to brown. Remove from oven and place on rack; let cool for 5 minutes.

Meanwhile prepare topping: In large bowl, combine granulated sugar, flour, baking powder, salt and zest. In small bowl, beat together lemon juice and eggs; stir into sugar mixture until smooth. Spread evenly over warm base.

Bake for 23 to 25 minutes or until top is set. Let cool in pan on rack. Just before serving, dust with icing sugar. Cut into bars. *(To store: Cover pan tightly and refrigerate for up to 2 days.)*

Makes 16 bars. PER BAR: 155 cal, 2 g pro, 8 g fat, 20 g carb.

Crispy Peanut Butter Marshmallow Squares

6	cups (1.5 L) crisp rice cereal
1	cup (250 mL) raisins
1	cup (250 mL) unsalted peanuts
1	cup (250 mL) unsalted sunflower seeds
¾	cup (175 mL) smooth peanut butter
½	cup (125 mL) butter, at room temperature
1	(400 g) package regular-size or miniature white marshmallows
1	teaspoon (5 mL) salt
1	teaspoon (5 mL) vanilla extract

In large bowl, combine cereal, raisins, peanuts and sunflower seeds.

In heavy 5-quart (5 L) pot, combine peanut butter and butter. Place over low to medium-low heat; stir until melted and blended. Add marshmallows and salt; stir until melted and blended. Remove from heat; stir in vanilla. Quickly stir in cereal mixture until well coated.

Using lightly buttered spatula, quickly spread mixture evenly and firmly into greased 13x9-inch (33x23 cm) baking pan. Let cool in pan on rack. Cut into squares.

Microwave Method: In 16 cup (4 L) microwaveable bowl, microwave peanut butter, butter, marshmallows and salt on High for 2 minutes and 45 seconds or until melted, stirring every minute. Remove bowl from microwave oven and stir until smooth. Stir in vanilla. Quickly stir in cereal mixture until well coated. Spread in greased baking pan.

Tip: *Use homogenized rather than natural peanut butter, which has a layer of oil on top.*

Makes 24 squares. PER SQUARE: 254 cal, 6 g pro, 14 g fat, 30 g carb.

Cranberry Butter Tart Squares

Base

1 ½ cups (375 mL) all-purpose flour
⅓ cup (75 mL) granulated sugar
¾ cup (175 mL) cold butter, cut into small pieces

Topping

2 large eggs
1 ¼ cups (300 mL) packed brown sugar
1 tablespoon (15 mL) golden corn syrup
2 tablespoons (30 mL) butter, melted
¼ teaspoon (1 mL) salt
1 teaspoon (5 mL) vanilla extract
1 teaspoon (5 mL) white vinegar
½ teaspoon (2 mL) baking powder
¼ cup (50 mL) quick-cooking oats (not instant), ground fine
¾ cup (175 mL) dried cranberries
½ cup (125 mL) walnuts, chopped

Base: In medium bowl, combine flour and granulated sugar. Using pastry blender, cut in butter until mixture resembles coarse crumbs. Press evenly onto bottom and 1 inch (2.5 cm) up sides of ungreased 9-inch (23 cm) square baking pan. Bake at 350 F (180 C) for 25 minutes or until light golden around edges, covering loosely with foil for the last 5 minutes of baking time. Let cool in pan on rack for 5 minutes.

Topping: In large bowl, whisk together eggs, brown sugar and corn syrup. Whisk in butter, salt, vanilla and vinegar. Whisk in baking powder. Stir in oats, cranberries and walnuts; spread evenly over warm base. Bake for 22 minutes or until golden and softly set. Let cool in pan on rack. Cut into squares. *(To store: Cover pan tightly and refrigerate for up to 3 days or transfer to airtight container and freeze for up to 2 weeks.)*

Makes 16 squares. PER SQUARE: 273 cal, 4 g pro, 13 g fat, 37 g carb.

Chocolate Drizzled Cherry Bars

Base

1	cup (250 mL) all-purpose flour
1	cup (250 mL) quick-cooking oats (not instant)
1	cup (250 mL) packed brown sugar
½	teaspoon (2 mL) baking soda
¼	teaspoon (1 mL) salt
½	cup (125 mL) butter, at room temperature

Filling

1 ¼	cups (300 mL) dried tart cherries, chopped coarse (about 7 ounces/200 g)
2	tablespoons (30 mL) kirsch
2	tablespoons (30 mL) all-purpose flour
1	teaspoon (5 mL) baking powder
½	teaspoon (2 mL) salt
2	large eggs
¾	cup (175 mL) packed brown sugar
½	teaspoon (2 mL) almond extract
1	cup (250 mL) sweetened medium coconut
½	cup (125 mL) pecans, chopped coarse

Topping

2	ounces (60 g) semi-sweet chocolate, chopped
1	teaspoon (5 mL) vegetable oil

Base: In medium bowl, combine flour, oats, sugar, soda and salt. Drop butter, in small pieces, on top of flour mixture; mix with fork and then fingers until crumbly. Press evenly into greased 13x9-inch (33x23 cm) baking pan. Bake at 350 F (180 C) for 10 minutes. Let cool in pan on rack.

Filling: In small bowl, soak cherries in kirsch for 30 minutes, stirring occasionally. In small bowl, combine flour, baking powder and salt.

In large bowl, beat eggs until frothy. Stir in sugar and almond extract. Stir in flour mixture. Stir in coconut and soaked cherries until well blended.

Pour filling over base and spread evenly. Sprinkle with pecans. Bake for 25 minutes or until lightly browned. Let cool in pan on rack.

Topping: Melt chocolate with oil. Using fork, drizzle chocolate over top of filling. Let chocolate set. Cut into bars.

Tip: Kirsch is an eau-de-vie — a clear, colourless brandy distilled from fruit juice. Kirsch is made from cherry juice.

Makes 30 bars. PER BAR: 168 cal, 2 g pro, 7 g fat, 26 g carb.

Grandma's Gingerbread Men (recipe on following page)

Christmas Baking

Grandma's Gingerbread Men

¼	cup (50 mL) finely chopped crystallized ginger
2	teaspoons (10 mL) all-purpose flour
½	cup (125 mL) butter, at room temperature
¼	cup (50 mL) plus 2 tablespoons (30 mL) fancy molasses
2	tablespoons (30 mL) golden corn syrup
1 ½	teaspoons (7 mL) ground ginger
½	teaspoon (2 mL) ground cinnamon
¼	teaspoon (1 mL) ground cloves
½	teaspoon (2 mL) baking soda
¼	teaspoon (1 mL) salt
1	cup (250 mL) packed brown sugar
1	large egg, well beaten
2 ½	cups (625 mL) all-purpose flour

Decorating icing

1	cup (250 mL) icing sugar
1	tablespoon (15 mL) butter, at room temperature
1 ½	tablespoons (22 mL) milk, about

In small bowl, combine crystallized ginger and 2 teaspoons (10 mL) flour; toss to coat.

In large (10-cup/2.5 L) heavy saucepan, combine butter, molasses and corn syrup.

In another small bowl, combine ground ginger, cinnamon, cloves, soda and salt. Stir in sugar until well blended; add to butter mixture. Place over medium heat and stir until mixture just comes to a boil. Remove from heat and stirring constantly, gradually add egg; stir until egg is well blended. Stir in about one-quarter of the flour. Stir in crystallized ginger. Add remaining flour, in 3 additions, stirring well after each addition; let dough stand at room temperature for 10 minutes. (Dough will be very soft and pliable.)

Meanwhile, line pie pan with plastic wrap, letting enough wrap extend over edge to completely cover dough. Scrape dough from saucepan into prepared pie pan; overwrap with plastic wrap to seal tightly. Refrigerate overnight or until firm enough to roll out, about 5 hours. *(Make ahead: Refrigerate for up to 3 days.)*

When ready to use, remove dough from refrigerator and let stand at room temperature for 15 minutes or until pliable enough to roll out.

On lightly floured surface, roll out dough until ¼-inch (5 mm) thick. Using 4¾-inch (12 cm) metal gingerbread man cookie cutter, cut into shapes. (Gather dough scraps and knead into smooth ball, then reroll and cut more cookies.) Place, 2 inches (5 cm) apart, on parchment-paper-lined rimless baking sheets.

Bake at 400 F (200 C) for 8 to 10 minutes or until puffed and set around edges. (Do not let edges of gingerbread men start to brown. Cookies will become firm when cool.) Let cool on baking sheet for 3 minutes, then transfer cookies to rack and let cool.

Icing: In medium bowl, beat sugar, butter and enough milk to make icing of piping consistency. Decorate gingerbread men with icing.

Tip: *Baking time will affect the texture of these cookies — less time results in a chewy cookie, while more time yields a crisp cookie. At 8 minutes, we turned out cookies just the way we like them — chewy in the centre and crisp around the edges. Experiment and bake one cookie to obtain an accurate timing for desired cookie texture.*

Makes 20 cookies. PER COOKIE: 194 cal, 2 g pro, 6 g fat, 34 g carb.

Vanilla Bean Shortbread Wedges

½   cup (125 mL) berry sugar (extra fine granulated sugar)
1   vanilla bean
1   cup (250 mL) butter, at room temperature
2   cups (500 mL) all-purpose flour

Place sugar in small bowl. With sharp knife, slit vanilla bean in half lengthwise and scrape out seeds; add seeds to sugar. Press mixture through fine sieve set over small bowl and stir to disperse seeds. Cut vanilla bean pieces, crosswise, in thirds and submerge in sugar. Cover bowl tightly and set aside for 1 to 2 weeks. (When ready to use, discard pieces of vanilla bean.)

In medium bowl, beat butter and vanilla-sugar until fluffy. Gradually stir in flour and mix until dough can be gathered into a ball.

On lightly floured surface, knead lightly until dough forms a smooth ball. Divide dough in half. Press each half into 5½-inch (14 cm) round, about ¾-inch (2 cm) thick. Place on ungreased rimless baking sheet. Using back of fork, lightly press edge of each round. With sharp knife, score top of each round into 8 wedges and prick dough all over with fork.

Bake at 275 F (140 C) for 50 to 60 minutes or until shortbread is pale golden around edges. Leave shortbread on baking sheet for 2 minutes, then cut into wedges and transfer to rack to cool.

For Cookies: Roll dough out until ⅜-inch (1 cm) thick. Cut into 2-inch (5 cm) rounds with cookie cutter; pierce each round twice with fork. Bake at 275 F (140 C) for about 40 minutes. Makes 28 cookies.

Tip: *Omit vanilla-sugar. Substitute 2 teaspoons (10 mL) pure vanilla extract for seeds. Beat extract into butter-sugar mixture before adding flour.*

Makes 16 wedges. PER WEDGE: 193 cal, 2 g pro, 12 g fat, 19 g carb.

Gingerbread Wedges

1 ¼	cups (300 mL) all-purpose flour
¾	teaspoon (4 mL) baking soda
½	teaspoon (2 mL) salt
1	teaspoon (5 mL) ground cinnamon
½	teaspoon (2 mL) ground ginger
¼	teaspoon (1 mL) ground cloves
½	cup (125 mL) buttermilk
½	cup (125 mL) fancy molasses
⅓	cup (75 mL) packed brown sugar
⅓	cup (75 mL) butter, at room temperature
1	large egg
2	tablespoons (30 mL) finely chopped, drained preserved ginger
	Icing sugar

Grease and flour 10-inch (25 cm) springform pan. In large bowl, combine flour, soda, salt, cinnamon, ground ginger and cloves.

In blender, blend buttermilk, molasses, brown sugar, butter and egg for 2 minutes. Add preserved ginger and blend until mixed; add to flour mixture and stir just until dry ingredients are moistened. Pour batter into prepared pan.

Bake at 350 F (180 C) for 30 minutes or until cake tester inserted in centre of gingerbread comes out clean. Let cool in pan on rack for 5 minutes, then remove side of pan and let cool. Just before serving, dust with icing sugar. Cut into wedges.

Makes 12 wedges. PER WEDGE: 170 cal, 2 g pro, 6 g fat, 28 g carb.

Any-Way-You-Like-It Shortbread

3 ¼	cups (800 mL) all-purpose flour
¾	cup (175 mL) cornstarch
2	cups (500 mL) butter, at room temperature
1	cup (250 mL) icing sugar

In medium bowl, combine flour and cornstarch. In large bowl, beat butter and sugar until fluffy. Gradually stir in flour mixture and mix until dough can be just gathered into a ball.

On lightly floured surface, knead lightly until dough forms a smooth ball. Divide dough in half. Press each half into a round, ¾-inch (2 cm) thick. Wrap each round in plastic wrap and refrigerate for 30 minutes.

On lightly floured surface, roll dough out until ⅜-inch (1 cm) thick. Cut into 1¾-inch (4.5 cm) rounds with cookie cutter. Place, 2 inches (5 cm) apart, on ungreased rimless baking sheets and pierce each round twice with fork. Refrigerate for 30 minutes.

Bake at 300 F (150 C) for 25 to 30 minutes or until pale golden on bottom and edges. Transfer cookies to rack and let cool.

Variations: After flour has been added to dough, mix in one of the following ingredients and knead lightly until dough forms a smooth ball.

- **Chocolate:** 6 tablespoons (90 mL) mini chocolate chips
- **Cranberry:** ¾ cup (175 mL) chopped dried cranberries
- **Ginger:** ¾ cup (175 mL) chopped crystallized ginger
- **Pistachio:** ¾ cup (175 mL) chopped, unsalted pistachios
- **Rosemary:** 3 tablespoons (45 mL) finely chopped fresh rosemary

Makes 54 cookies. PER COOKIE: 107 cal, 1 g pro, 7 g fat, 10 g carb.

Chocolate Hazelnut Shortbread Stars

3 ¼	cups (800 mL) all-purpose flour
¾	cup (175 mL) cornstarch
1	cup (250 mL) hazelnuts, toasted and chopped very fine
¼	teaspoon (1 mL) salt
2	cups (500 mL) butter, at room temperature
1	cup (250 mL) icing sugar
½	teaspoon (2 mL) vanilla extract
2	ounces (60 g) semi-sweet chocolate, chopped coarse
2	teaspoons (10 mL) vegetable oil, divided
2	ounces (60 g) white chocolate, chopped coarse

In large bowl, combine flour, cornstarch, hazelnuts and salt. In another large bowl, beat butter and sugar until fluffy. Beat in vanilla. Gradually stir in flour mixture and mix until dough can be just gathered into a ball.

On lightly floured surface, knead lightly until dough forms a smooth ball. Divide dough in half. Press each half into a round, ¾-inch (2 cm) thick. Wrap each round in plastic wrap and refrigerate for 45 minutes.

On lightly floured surface, roll out each half of dough until ⅜-inch (1 cm) thick. Cut into 1¾-inch (4.5 cm) star shapes with metal cookie cutter. Place, 2 inches (5 cm) apart, on ungreased rimless baking sheets and pierce each star twice with fork. Refrigerate for 30 minutes.

Bake at 300 F (150 C) for 25 to 28 minutes or until pale golden on bottom and edges. Transfer cookies to rack and let cool.

Melt semi-sweet chocolate with 1 teaspoon (5 mL) oil. Using fork, drizzle semi-sweet chocolate over each cookie. Melt white chocolate with remaining 1 teaspoon (5 mL) oil; drizzle over each cookie. Let chocolate set.

Makes 60 cookies. PER COOKIE: 119 cal, 1 g pro, 9 g fat, 10 g carb.

Triple Chocolate Shortbread Drops

2 ½	cups (625 mL) all-purpose flour
2	cups (500 mL) butter, at room temperature
1	cup (250 mL) berry sugar (extra fine granulated sugar)
1	cup (250 mL) rice flour
½	cup (125 mL) coarsely chopped bittersweet chocolate
½	cup (125 mL) coarsely chopped milk chocolate
½	cup (125 mL) coarsely chopped white chocolate
1	cup (250 mL) pecans, chopped coarse

Spread all-purpose flour on rimmed baking sheet. Broil 4 inches (10 cm) from heat source for 7 to 11 minutes, stirring when flour just begins to turn golden in spots, about every 3 minutes. Let cool.

In large bowl, beat butter and sugar until fluffy. Beat in rice flour and cooled all-purpose flour. Stir in bittersweet chocolate, milk chocolate, white chocolate and pecans.

Drop dough by heaping tablespoonfuls (15 mL), 2 inches (5 cm) apart, onto parchment-paper-lined or ungreased rimless baking sheets.

Bake at 300 F (150 C) for 25 to 30 minutes or until golden on bottom and edges. Transfer cookies to rack and let cool.

Tip: *Broiling the flour adds a delicious nutty flavour to these cookies. If you're pressed for time, omit this step — the cookies won't be quite as rich in flavour but we're sure no one will complain.*

Makes 52 cookies. PER COOKIE: 160 cal, 1 g pro, 11 g fat, 15 g carb.

Christmas Macaroons

1	cup (250 mL) berry sugar (extra fine granulated sugar)
1	tablespoon (15 mL) cornstarch
⅛	teaspoon (0.5 mL) salt
3	large egg whites
1	cup (250 mL) unsweetened flaked coconut
½	cup (125 mL) candied (glacé) red or green cherries, chopped fine
¼	cup (50 mL) finely chopped candied (glacé) pineapple
¼	cup (50 mL) whole blanched almonds, chopped

In small bowl, combine sugar, cornstarch and salt. In large bowl, beat egg whites until stiff peaks form. Very gradually add sugar mixture to egg whites, beating constantly. Transfer mixture to top of double boiler set over hot water. Cook on low heat for 8 minutes or until mixture is warm and sugar has dissolved, stirring constantly.

Remove from heat; fold in coconut, cherries, pineapple and almonds. Drop by tablespoonfuls (15 mL), 2 inches (5 cm) apart, onto parchment-paper-lined rimless baking sheets.

Bake at 300 F (150 C) for 20 to 30 minutes or until light golden. Transfer cookies to rack and let cool. *(Do not freeze these cookies.)*

Pine Nut Variation: Omit candied cherries, pineapple and almonds. Fold in ½ cup (125 mL) pine nuts along with the coconut.

Makes 40 cookies. PER COOKIE: 54 cal, 1 g pro, 2 g fat, 9 g carb.

Mexican Wedding Cakes

1	cup (250 mL) butter, at room temperature
2	cups (500 mL) icing sugar, divided
¼	teaspoon (1 mL) salt
½	teaspoon (2 mL) vanilla extract
2	cups (500 mL) all-purpose flour
1	cup (250 mL) walnuts, chopped fine

In large bowl, beat butter, ½ cup (125 mL) sugar, salt and vanilla until fluffy. Stir in flour to make a stiff dough. Stir in walnuts. Divide dough in half and press each half into a round, ¾-inch (2 cm) thick. Wrap each round in plastic wrap and refrigerate overnight or until chilled, about 45 minutes.

Shape dough into 1-inch (2.5 cm) balls. Place, 2 inches (5 cm) apart, on parchment-paper-lined or ungreased rimless baking sheets.

Bake at 400 F (200 C) for 8 to 10 minutes or until very pale golden. Transfer cookies to rack and let cool for 3 minutes. While still warm, roll cookies, one at a time, in bowl with remaining 1½ cups (375 mL) sugar, until evenly coated. Return to rack and let cool.

When cookies are completely cool, reroll in remaining sugar. If desired, sift some extra icing sugar over cookies before serving.

Tip: *If possible, before purchasing walnuts, taste one and make sure it's not bitter or starting to go rancid.*

Makes 44 cookies. PER COOKIE: 99 cal, 1 g pro, 6 g fat, 10 g carb.

Brandy Fruitcake Bites

1 ½   cups (375 mL) diced candied (glacé) mixed fruit
½   cup (125 mL) dried currants
½   cup (125 mL) raisins
      Brandy
1   cup (250 mL) all-purpose flour
¼   teaspoon (1 mL) baking powder
½   teaspoon (2 mL) ground cinnamon
¼   teaspoon (1 mL) ground cloves
¼   teaspoon (1 mL) ground mace
½   cup (125 mL) butter, at room temperature
½   cup (125 mL) packed brown sugar
2   large eggs
¼   cup (50 mL) fancy molasses
¼   cup (50 mL) liquid honey
1   cup (250 mL) pecans, chopped
14   candied (glacé) red or green cherries, quartered (for decorating)

In medium bowl, combine mixed fruit, currants and raisins. Stir in 3 tablespoons (45 mL) brandy. Cover tightly; let stand overnight.

In small bowl, combine flour, baking powder, cinnamon, cloves and mace. In large bowl, beat butter and sugar until fluffy. Beat in eggs, one at a time. Beat in molasses and honey (batter may appear curdled). Beat in flour mixture. Stir in fruit mixture and pecans.

Place paper candy cups (1½ inches/4 cm in diameter across the top) on rimmed baking sheets. Fill with batter; top each with piece of cherry.

Bake at 300 F (150 C) for 25 minutes or until cake springs back when lightly pressed with fingertip. Remove from oven; brush each fruitcake with brandy. Transfer to rack; let cool. Store overnight before serving.

Makes 54 fruitcake bites. PER BITE: 86 cal, 1 g pro, 4 g fat, 13 g carb.

Chocolate Amaretto Espresso Balls

2 ½   cups (625 mL) fine chocolate-wafer crumbs
1   cup (250 mL) icing sugar
1   cup (250 mL) lightly packed ground almonds
3 ½   ounces (100 g) bittersweet chocolate, ground
¼   teaspoon (1 mL) salt
2   teaspoons (10 mL) instant espresso coffee powder
½   cup (125 mL) amaretto
2   tablespoons (30 mL) golden corn syrup
¼   cup (50 mL) very soft (not melted) butter
⅔   cup (150 mL) semi-sweet chocolate sprinkles, about

In medium bowl, combine crumbs, sugar, almonds, bittersweet chocolate and salt. In small bowl, dissolve coffee powder in amaretto. Stir in corn syrup.

Drop butter, in small pieces, over top of crumb mixture. Pour amaretto mixture over top; using fork, stir until blended. Immediately form crumb mixture into 1 ¼-inch (3 cm) balls. After shaping each ball, roll immediately in sprinkles to coat.

Tips

- *One (200 g) package wafers yields about 2 ½ cups (625 mL) fine crumbs. Process wafers in food processor to form fine crumbs.*
- *Chop bittersweet chocolate, then finely grind in food processor.*
- *For best flavour, buy real chocolate not "chocolate-flavoured" sprinkles. Four ounces (125 g) chocolate sprinkles will yield about ⅔ cup (150 mL).*

Makes 48 balls. PER BALL: 82 cal, 1 g pro, 4 g fat, 11 g carb.

Index

About the Nutritional Analysis

• The approximate nutritional analysis for each recipe does not include variations or optional ingredients.

• Figures are rounded off.

• Abbreviations: cal = calories, pro = protein, carb = carbohydrate